RUDOLF STEINER (1861–1925) called his spiritual philosophy 'anthroposophy', meaning 'wisdom of the human being'. As a highly developed seer, he based his work on direct knowledge and perception of spiritual dimensions. He initiated a modern and universal 'science of spirit', accessible to anyone willing to exercise clear and unprejudiced thinking.

From his spiritual investigations Steiner provided suggestions for the renewal of many activities, including education (both general and special), agriculture, medicine, economics, architecture, science, philosophy, religion and the arts. Today there are thousands of schools, clinics, farms and other organizations involved in practical work based on his principles. His many published works feature his research into the spiritual nature of the human being, the evolution of the world and humanity, and methods of personal development. Steiner wrote some 30 books and delivered over 6000 lectures across Europe. In 1924 he founded the General Anthroposophical Society, which today has branches throughout the world.

THE NIGHT

as a Wellspring of Strength

Sleep, Spiritual Encounters and the Starry Firmament

RUDOLF STEINER

Selected and compiled by Edward de Boer

RUDOLF STEINER PRESS

Translated by Matthew Barton

Rudolf Steiner Press,
Hillside House, The Square
Forest Row, RH18 5ES

www.rudolfsteinerpress.com

Published by Rudolf Steiner Press 2018

Originally published in German under the title *Die Nacht als Kraftquelle* by Futurum Verlag, Basel, in 2013

A catalogue record for this book is available from the British Library

Print book ISBN: 978 1 85584 544 2
Ebook ISBN: 978 1 85584 500 8

Cover by Morgan Creative
Typeset by DP Photosetting, Neath, West Glamorgan
Printed and bound by 4Edge Ltd., Essex

Contents

Introduction

All of us have a picture of the night, as we do of the daytime. The night is a realm of quiet, when we are—usually—asleep. Each of us has a personal relationship with night-time, with sleep and the images of dream life, or with the starry heavens to which we raise our conscious gaze. The stars appear to many of us as the mysterious harbingers of an expansive, light-filled world.

Anthroposophy can help illumine for us this star-sown realm of wisdom, the world of the night, accompanying us through its vivid and encompassing realities.

In his lectures and teachings Rudolf Steiner pointed repeatedly to the significance of the night, and it acquires central importance in various esoteric exercises. One fundamental exercise in the anthroposophic path of schooling, for instance, is the 'review of the day' undertaken in the evening, before and in preparation for sleep. Further meditative exercises start here too, often involving a two-part practice to be done in the evening and then the following morning, as prelude to, and then fading away of, night-time experience.

It is a key tenet of anthroposophy that the night, when we sleep, is an essential counterpart to the day. By day we possess the capacity of conscious, logical thinking, while at night, leaving the physical body to regenerate, we give ourselves up to a quite different form of consciousness. Steiner describes night-time as the realm of intuition, a place of deep spiritual encounter, but also as a wellspring of renewal and healing.

For initiates, as we learn both from the ancient mysteries and from modern initiation science, the night is a field of conscious awareness, becoming illumined if we can acquire supersensible consciousness within it. Just as we can learn to see better in the dark, so an inner light can gradually dawn on us during the night. In the mysteries of ancient times this capacity to perceive bright spiritual realities was called 'seeing the sun at midnight'. Waking life during the day, and this distinctive form of night consciousness, complement and enlarge each other. In supersensible vision, day and night consciousness become one.

Rudolf Steiner describes the night as a realm important for poetic and artistic inspiration. The idea for a new work of art can emerge from the quiet of the night. Someone able to hearken to the harmonies of the planets at night-time encounters spheres described by Pythagoras in his mystery school, and new kinds of musical experience can originate there.

In the night, finally, we also consciously or unconsciously meet our higher self, our 'genius'. In converse with our spirit self we can, quite literally, find inspiration that gives wings to our daily work. Consciously readying ourselves for the night before we fall asleep is a preparation for this encounter. In a lecture which Steiner gave in Berlin in 1917 he describes how we can picture this:

I fall asleep. Until I awaken my soul will be in the world of spirit, and there will meet the guiding impulse-giver of my earthly life, my genius, who dwells in the world of spirit, hovering round my head. And when I awaken once more, I will have met my genius, and have felt upon my soul the beating of his wings.[1]

The night is therefore a realm where we meet real beings: not only our own higher self, our genius, but other beings too, in either conscious or unconscious encounter. But only a conscious experience of the night can illumine for us the diverse dimensions of these spiritual encounters. In many of his lectures, Steiner described how the spirit or angelic hierarchies work upon our human nature. The angels, along with other spiritual beings, work upon us formatively at night, giving our sleep an upbuilding, regenerating, renewing potency.

The world of the dead, too, is close to us at night. Chiefly at the transitional moments of falling asleep and awakening it is possible for us to develop a conscious and inspiring relationship with dead souls. A loving, meditative contemplation of the relationship we had with each person who has passed away can open up for us a special realm in which they can approach us at these intermediate moments, for instance answering a question we put to them the evening before as we fell asleep.

The moon and stars are emblematic of night. As we gaze upon the starry firmament, both the fixed stars and the planets, a hidden script can become visible to us. Rudolf Steiner often describes the living, spirit-filled images which ancient cultures (of Egypt or Chaldea) perceived in the constellations, and emphasizes the living reality of these 'intelligences'. In a lecture he gave in 1924, he says that each of us has our own star, our luminous spiritual home and origin.

In many verses and prayers concerning the night and the stars, Steiner makes this world of spirit and light accessible to us. Here he clothes the night-time realm of stars in meditative words so that we can more easily contemplate and immerse ourselves in it. Sometimes, in an exercise intended for a particular person, for example, the night with its constellations forms a bridge leading the meditant on the path of initiation to his own higher self. Of these verses, I'd like to mention one in particular, which Rudolf Steiner wrote in 1915 for the mother of a soldier killed in battle. After the death of her son she was plunged into despair, and the verse comforts and guides her towards the world of light and hope. The bright stars here become sustaining powers of the soul.

This compilation seeks first and foremost to conjure the special atmosphere and quality of the night and vividly convey this. The choice of passages, lecture extracts, exercises and verses is intended as an invitation to readers to engage more consciously and luminously with the nightly realm, accompanying each person on their own unique developing path and relationship with it.

For a fuller and more systematic account of night-time experience and schooling, the two books *Knowledge of the Higher Worlds* and *Occult Science, an Outline* are very helpful.[2] And for more on the evening review exercise, see the volume in this series, *Strengthening the Will, the Review Exercises,* which offers an excellent survey of this field.[3]

In Chapter 1 we first enter into the mood of the night,

meeting 'images and impressions' connected with it, as a prelude to the theme as a whole. At the same time certain modes of perception of night-time experience are introduced. We also hear what diverse thinkers and poets—Kant, Novalis, Goethe—have to say about it. Steiner describes the different connection each of these figures has with this realm, at the same time elaborating on the night as a deep source of inspiration. Chapter 2 moves on to describe how, specifically, a 'night consciousness' can be developed, and what experiences arise in consequence. The following chapter takes us further into sleep as, in many respects, our primary 'source of renewal and healing'. Each night, sleep refreshes and regenerates us, not least also because the higher levels of our being, or higher bodies, are working unconsciously upon our physical and etheric body.

The chapter on 'Spiritual Encounters' concerns the many meetings with other beings we have during sleep at night, whether consciously or unconsciously: elemental beings, and beings of the angelic hierarchies, our own 'genius' and souls of the dead with whom we are connected. These encounters, the 'social' aspect of the night, work unconsciously upon our destiny for the coming day.

The chapter on 'The Starry Firmament' directs our gaze to the heavens and the cosmos. The passages collected here show how we can develop our own intimate relationship to the spiritual dimension of the stars and planets. The next chapter, too, 'Sacred and Holy Nights', concerns the cosmic dimension of existence, not only describing *the* Holy Night which we know and celebrate as Christmas Eve, but the whole Christmas period as a sacred time. In the twelve holy nights, as they are known, we can develop an inner, spiritual relationship with the cosmos.

The chapter on 'Meditations as Prelude and Epilogue to the Night' offers a range of schooling exercises concerned with preparation for night-time experience and integration of it the next morning, and at the same time a survey of the diverse ways in which we can approach such experiences. Some of these citations are drawn from the Esoteric School or a related context, and were not therefore originally intended for publication. But above and beyond their original context, they show how we can employ the evening and morning as special moments of transition which help us to form a more conscious spiritual connection with the realm of night. We have also included here a three-part exercise spanning meditative work not only in the evening and morning but also at the moment of midday.

The last chapter of this little 'guidebook' collects verses and prayers for nightly mindfulness, with an emphasis on experiencing the stars and lights of heaven. The chapter also offers a survey of the wealth of verses which Steiner conceived for, and gave to, specific individuals. Despite this, in retrospect and in the context of this compilation, they acquire meaning above and beyond the lives of their original recipients.

As the title suggests, *The Night as a Wellspring of Strength* is intended as a source of inspiration and a companion on the journey through the mysterious world of the night. The real spiritual encounters of the night can in turn fruitfully inform our daily life and help us to live in a fuller, healthier way.

Edward de Boer

1. Images and Impressions of the Night

Tranquil blue around me everywhere,
quiet peace in my soul.
The spirits of the universe say to me:

Let the stars shine
within your human body—
luminous stars,
warming stars.

(For Emmy Thurnheer, August 1924[4])

I stand upright in star-bright night and gaze at the starry firmament, allowing the impression to work upon me. And if a person has the capacity for this, what lives in the patterns of the constellations, in the movements of the planets, transforms into a great cosmic script. Reading this script, something emerges of the kind I described yesterday when speaking of the secrets of the moon. These are things that can be read in the inscriptions of the cosmos when the stars are no longer merely something mathematically and mechanically quantifiable, but have become for you the letters of a universal script.
(Dornach, 22 April 1924[5])

Worship of the stars, worship of the night as we can also say—since often the matter was veiled to make the night itself the object of veneration rather than the starry firmament—

held sway amongst peoples with an inclination for thinking. For ancient peoples with a thinking, ruminating nature, religions were founded through which they learned of the origin of their thinking and its instrument, their head. And many of the names borne by the most ancient gods of certain peoples can only be translated into later languages as 'the night'. The night itself, appearing as mysterious mother of the stars, from whose womb the stars emerge, was worshipped because esoteric initiates knew that the instrument of the brain truly does originate in the star-strewn night. *(Kristiania (Oslo), 9 June 1912[6])*

We can look at the world, really, from two perspectives. One arises when, say, someone observes a very beautiful sunrise, with the sun giving birth to itself, it seems, out of the red gold of dawn, then lifting brilliantly above the earth. At such moments we can immerse ourselves in the thought of the sun's rays, the sun's warmth, conjuring life from the earth, from the ground, in the ever-recurring cycle of the year. But another contemplation appears when the sun has set and its afterglow has faded from the sky, giving way gradually to the darkness of night in which the pinpricks of countless stars start to shine in the firmament. Then we can immerse ourselves in the miracle of the starry sky at night. And gazing on this, we can form a thought which, closely resembling a primary, Goethean idea, inevitably fills us with the profoundest bliss. Ah, when we direct our gaze upward to the miracle of the starry world, and contemplate the unfolding universe with all its glories, ultimately we can feel that all of this, everything appearing so gloriously around us in the whole compass of the cosmos, only gains its true meaning when mirrored in a marvelling human being, a human soul. *(Hanover, 27 December 1911[7])*

Kant says something very beautiful. Two things, he says, have made a very striking impression on me: the starry heavens above me and the moral law within me. And the impression is heightened still further when we recognize that these two things are one, for between death and rebirth we are poured out through starry space and absorb its powers. And when we are in a physical body again, these powers we absorbed come to effect in us as our moral impulses. When we stand here and gaze up at the stars we can say that what lives outside us up there, weaving in cosmic space, is a realm in which we ourselves live and weave in the period between death and rebirth. And this now becomes the guiding lawfulness of our moral life. Thus the starry heavens outside us and the moral law within us are indeed one and the same reality, merely two different aspects of it. Between death and a new birth we inhabit the starry firmament, and between birth and death moral law inhabits us here on earth.

If we comprehend this, spiritual science leads us directly to reverence, as to a mighty prayer—for what is a prayer other than what unites our soul with the divine spirit weaving through the world?

This prayer is what a prayer can be for us today. We have to master it by working our way through the sense world. By consciously aspiring to this, what we can know in consequence becomes prayer quite by itself. Spiritual insight becomes direct feeling, experience and impression, and should indeed do so. However much such knowledge works with concepts and ideas, ultimately ideas and concepts become pure, prayerful impressions and feelings. And that is what our era needs. The age we live in needs thoughts and reflections to flow directly out into felt experience of the cosmos, where they become prayerful.

(Bern, 15 December 1912[8])

Novalis was able to see that waking life during the day, with its mundane consciousness, is only part of the experience of contemporary humanity; and that every soul, immersing itself at night in unconsciousness, is in fact plunging into a spiritual world. He was able to feel profoundly, and to know, that in these worlds of spirit in which the soul is plunged at night, a higher spiritual reality exists; and that the day with all its sense impressions, even those of sun and light, is only a small part of the totality of spiritual reality. The stars, as it were stealthily sending down during the night the light of the day, appeared to him only as a faint gleam compared to the truth of the spirit dawning in his awareness, as it dawns on the seer in the blinding bright astral light when his waking spirit can travel into the realm of night. Thus the worlds of the night, the true world of spirit, dawn on Novalis and make the night precious to him.

(Berlin, 26 October 1908[9])

On a beautiful day we wait until nightfall, then gaze up at the dome of the heavens, seeing the many luminous patterns of stars glittering across its whole expanse. The soul finds a new jubilance: the descent from above of something that kindles in us joyful, inward rejoicing.

Thus in the daytime we can look upon the colourful tapestry of the earth's growing plants, in perceptions that fill us with joy. And then, at night, we can look up to the heavens that appear blue by day but now are strewn with sparkling, gleaming stars, and can rejoice inwardly at what descends from above to reveal itself in our soul. This holds true for our ordinary awareness.

But having developed a form of consciousness that is empty but wakeful, into which the spiritual world has broken, then, when we gaze upon the plant covering of the earth, and look up at night to the gleaming, shining stars, we will say: Yes, during the day the colourful tapestry of plants and flowers enticed us and filled us with joy. But what did we actually see? And now, at night, we look up to the starry heights and the stars no longer merely gleam before this empty, alert awareness we now have—empty, that is, as regards the earth. Now the stars assume the most manifold forms and figures. The stars have ceased to merely sparkle, and we perceive there something wondrously essential and full of being. Spread across the heavens we see growing, weaving life, majestic, mighty and lofty. And we stand in acknowledging reverence, in reverent acknowledgement and perception. Yes, we have attained an intermediate stage of initiation, and we can say: only now is the plant world there above us. The true beings of the plants are apparent now in what previously only shone down to us as separate points of light. It now seems to us that the real plant world is there above us—as if the violet no longer appears as a violet but as if, when we see the violet in the early morning bearing a single drop of shining dew, we see only that drop of dew and not the violet. If we look at just a single star, now this single drop of dew sparkles in it. In truth, a mighty, weaving world of being lies behind it, and we are gazing toward it. Now we know what the plant world really is—it is not on the earth at all but out there in the cosmos; it is magnificent and mighty and noble and great. And what did we see, by day, in the colourful tapestry of plants? The mirror image of what lives above.

And now we see that the cosmos, with the weaving life of its forms, its living figures of beings, is mirrored on the earth. The earth's surface is a mirror. When we look in a mirror we know that we're seeing our reflection. Our outer form is reflected in the mirror. The soul is not directly visible. The heavens are not mirrored in the earth's surface in quite such a complete way, but as the yellow, green, blue, red and white shimmering colours of the plant world: these are a reflection of the heavens, a weak, shadowy one. And thus we come to know a new world. Above, the plants are humans, beings with self-awareness. And alongside the ordinary physical world and the astral world, we have a third world, a spiritual world as such. The stars are really like drops of dew, cosmic dewdrops from this world. Our plants are a reflection of this world. As we see them here below they are not everything that constitutes them. In fact in the form in which they appear to us on earth they are not even a being, but merely the reflection of an infinite fullness and depth of intense reality that exists up there in the world of spirit as such, from which the separate stars gleam forth as cosmic dewdrops. We have a third world, the spiritual world *per se*, and now we know that the whole glorious tapestry of plants only mirrors this world.

(Torquay, 12 August 1924[10])

The more I turn my gaze up to the stars in the night sky, the more I see the true being and essence of what lives there. Nature becomes whole when I look up from the earth to the stars and see the cosmos and the earth as one. And then I look back upon my human being, recognizing that I have compressed within me on earth what in the plant extends upward to those expanses. I bear within me as human being the physical, astral and spiritual world.

To comprehend this, to grow with nature up to the heights of the heavens, and to grow inward into the human being to the point where the heavens open in us, means raising ourselves to spiritual enquiry.

(Torquay, 12 August 1924[11])

When a person immerses himself in dreams in the stillness of the night, and when he has accustomed himself for a while to perceive quite different worlds, the time soon arrives when he learns also to step outward into reality with these new perceptions. And then this whole world acquires a new appearance for him. He becomes aware of this new aspect in the same way that we are aware of the sense world when we walk past these rows of chairs here, past everything that you see here. He is now in a new state of consciousness; something new, essential opens within him. And then a person progresses further in his development, at last coming to a point where he not only perceives the distinctive phenomena

of higher worlds, like light phenomena, with his spiritual gaze, but also hears resounding the tones of higher worlds so that things speak their spiritual names and come toward him with new significance. In the language of the mysteries this is called 'seeing the sun at midnight'; that is, there are no longer physical hindrances preventing him seeing the sun on the other side of the globe. And then he also comprehends what the sun does in cosmic space: and will be able to hear what the Pythagoreans propounded as a truth, the harmony of the spheres. This sounding and resounding, this harmony of the spheres, becomes reality for him. Poets who were also seers knew that the harmony of the spheres really exists. This is the only way in which we can properly understand Goethe. His words in the 'Prologue in Heaven', for example, can either be taken as empty poeticism or as—what they are—a higher truth. And in Part II of *Faust*, where the eponymous hero is conducted into the world of spirits, he speaks once again of this: 'For ears of spirit now the new day's born / with sounding resonance and tone.'
(Berlin, 5 October 1905[12])

This is an esoteric picture: to see the sun at midnight. At the moment the chela or pupil becomes clairvoyant, he looks through the earth and sees the sun. But it is a still grander thing to hear the sun resound. [. . .] The trumpets mentioned by John in the *Apocalypse* are a reality to the occultist.
(Leipzig, 10 November 1906[13])

When a person learns to perceive something of what he otherwise only sees as *maya* in the action of chemical compounds and solutions, he hears these spirits of movement, and perceives the music of the spheres, of which the Pythagorean and other mystery schools speak. This is also what Goethe describes when he speaks of the sun not as light-giver but in these words: 'The sun sounds forth its ancient tones, in rival song with brother spheres, completing with a thunderous motion, the destined circuit of its years.'

This music of the spheres is still present today, but inaudible to ordinary consciousness. It is a reality approaching all people from without as astral effect. People just don't hear it. If they underwent the same kind of change in relation to the music of the spheres as they do with light— seeing nothing when darkness falls—then they would also hear it at certain times. But it is sounding day and night, and they only therefore hear it by undergoing an esoteric training. Whereas light streams toward us during the day and weaves further at night as absorbed light, the music of the spheres resounds both day and night. In this respect a person is like the miller who only hears the sound of the mill when it falls quiet.

(Kristiania (Oslo), 11 June 1910[14])

2. Night Consciousness

In tranquil quest
in light-aspiring
life of soul
my I bears me
toward the source
from which human beings
draw their true essence.

(Handwritten note, undated[15])

It is for good reason that I ... have said that we really possess twelve senses. We must conceive of them in these terms: that a number of them are turned toward sensory things, while others are directed backwards. In our lower sphere they are also directed toward what is already reversed. The following senses are turned outward to the sense world: the sense of I, of thinking, of speech, of hearing, of vision, of taste, and smell. The others do not come to our awareness really because they are initially directed into our interior, and then toward the obverse of the world. These are primarily the sense of warmth, of life, of balance, of movement, and touch. And so we can say that, for ordinary awareness, seven of the senses are in the light and five lie in the dark. And these five senses in the dark are turned toward the other aspect of the world, also within us.

... Let us assume these senses therefore: the sense of hearing, speech, thinking, I, warmth, life, balance, movement, touch, smell, taste and vision. Basically everything from the sense of I to the sense of smell lies in the light, in what is available to ordinary awareness. And everything that is turned away from this ordinary awareness, as the night is the obverse of the day, belongs to the other senses. But this division of the human senses produces a schema that we can also equate with the heavenly constellations, thus: Aries, Taurus, Gemini, Cancer, Leo, Virgo and Libra—seven constellations for the bright aspect; then five for the dark: Scorpio, Sagittarius, Capricorn, Aquarius, Pisces. Thus: day, night, night, day. And this gives a complete parallelism between the microcosmic human being—between what is turned towards conscious sensing, and what is turned away from it, but is in fact turned toward our lower senses—and the alternation of day and night in the macrocosm. In a sense we can say that day and night alternate in us, in sleep and waking, as they do in the cosmos, although in our present cycle of consciousness these two things have emancipated themselves from each other. During the day we are turned toward the day-bright senses .... At night, like the aspect of earth which is turned away from the sun, we are turned toward the other senses. But these are not yet fully developed. Only after the Venus period will they have evolved fully so as to perceive what lies toward the other side. They are veiled in night, as the earth is wrapped in night as it passes through the other heavenly regions, through the other zodiac constellations. Our passage through our senses can be fully equated with the course of the sun round the earth or, if you like, of the earth round the sun—which for these purposes are the same. Yes, these things are connected.

(Dornach, 25 August 1918[16])

Look for a moment upon this mystery lying behind things. The night belongs to the moon, and did so to a much greater degree still at that ancient period before human beings were able to receive the power of love from the sun; before they could directly receive this power of love in the light. Back then they received the reflected power of mature wisdom from moonlight. It streamed toward them from the moonlight during the period of night consciousness.
(Hamburg, 20 May 1908[17])

Three states of consciousness exist, but ordinarily people are fully aware of only one of these, and this is because in the other two states they are unaware of themselves, and live in them without bringing any memory, any conscious effect of them through into the one state of consciousness of which they are aware. The latter is the state of consciousness we call ordinary, day-waking consciousness. The second is known to us to some degree, as dream-filled sleep, this painter in symbols who often merely presents us with symbols of our daily experiences. The third state of consciousness is dreamless sleep, which ordinarily signifies for people a kind of empty or void condition.

Initiation transforms the three states of consciousness. First of all our dream life alters, becomes less chaotic and no longer just a representation of daily experiences in a flux of often confused symbols. Instead a new world opens before us in dreaming sleep, one full of surging colours, full of shimmering beings of light that surrounds us: the astral world. Rather than some newly created world, this is new only to someone who previously has not gone beyond the lower state of daytime awareness. This world is always present in fact, continually surrounding us. It is a real world, just as real as the physical environment we perceive as reality. Once initiated, a person learns to perceive this wondrous world. He learns to live consciously within it, with as clear—no clearer—an awareness as his waking mind. He also becomes acquainted with his own astral body and learns to live consciously within it.

In this new world opening before him he witnesses a living, weaving, being-filled world of colour and light. After initiation a person begins to awaken from ordinary dreaming sleep as if lifted out of a surging ocean of flowing light and colours. And these surging colours, this shimmering light, are living beings. These experiences in conscious dream-sleep pass over also into his whole daily, waking life and awareness, so that he learns to see these beings in this waking state too.

A person achieves the third state of consciousness when he becomes able to transform dreamless sleep into a conscious condition. Again, the world in which he learns to enter dawns on him only partially to begin with, and then increasingly does so. He lives longer and longer in this condition, is conscious within it and there has very significant experiences.

Someone can develop perception of the second state, the astral world, by passing through what is called the 'great stillness'. He has to become still, completely still in himself. This great tranquillity has to precede awakening in the astral world. And this profoundest stillness grows ever greater as he begins to approach the third state of consciousness, of experiencing within dreamless sleep. The colours of the astral world become ever more transparent, the light ever clearer, as if more spiritualized. A person feels then as if he himself lives in this colour and light, as if, rather than it surrounding him, he himself has become this light and this colour. He feels himself to be astral within this astral world, as if swimming in great, deep tranquillity. And then this deep stillness slowly starts to resound, beginning to sound forth spiritually first softly then ever more audibly. It seems that the world of light and colour is infused with resounding tones. This third state of consciousness, into which we gradually enter, is one in which the colour world in which we lived in the astral realm is permeated with tone. And this is Devachan, called also the mental world, which now opens before us. We enter this wondrous world through the gateway of the great stillness; and from the great stillness tone resounds to us from the other world. This really is the nature of the world of Devachan.

(Berlin, 12 November 1906[18])

During the day, from the moment of waking to falling asleep, we always bear within us the echoes and after-effects of our night-time experiences. And though everything we consciously accomplish in life is of great significance for outward culture, what occurs within us is scarcely dependent at all on our consciousness but very largely results from what we unconsciously experience during sleep.

As sense perceptions gradually dull to nothing, as will impulses cease to act, we first experience an undifferentiated inner state. This is a generalized, indefinite state, an experience in which there is a clear feeling of time but with our sense of spatial conditions almost entirely extinguished.

We really can compare this experience with a kind of swimming, a kind of moving through a general, vague cosmic substance. We have to coin new expressions, really, to describe what the soul experiences here. The soul experiences itself as a wave in a great ocean, but an inwardly structured wave, which feels itself surrounded everywhere by the rest of the ocean, perceiving the actions of this ocean upon it as, in waking life, we feel, perceive and reflect upon the differentiated impressions of colours or tones, or conditions of heat upon us. But in contrast to waking experience, when we feel ourselves to be a person enclosed in our skin and standing at a particular place, at this moment after falling asleep we feel ... like a wave in a general ocean, sometimes here, sometimes there, and as I said, a particularized sense of space ceases. But a general sense of time remains. Yet this experience is connected with another, of being forsaken. It is as if we sank into an abyss. Without due preparation, a person who consciously experienced this first stage of sleep would find it unendurable to lose almost completely the sense of space and live only in a general feeling of time, to feel himself so undefined and only incorporated into a generalized, substantial ocean within which very little can be distinguished—only that one is a self in a generalized cosmic existence. If he became conscious of this, he would literally feel as if hovering over an abyss. In turn this is connected with something that surfaces in the soul as a huge need to be protected by a spiritual realm, a huge need to be sustained by and connected to spirit. In this generalized ocean in which we swim, we have in a certain way lost that sense of safety given by connection with material things of the waking world. And

for this reason we feel—or would do if the condition were conscious—a deep yearning for connection with the divine, spiritual realm. We can also put it like this: we experience this general moving through an undifferentiated cosmic substance as the security of living within divine spirit.
(Stuttgart, 9 October 1922[19])

A person really should occasionally enter into more inward communion with his spirit self, with the spirit self that becomes visible in the astral aura in the way I suggested, existing there as predisposition, not something that has been developed; which is, as it were overshone from above, from futurity. From time to time a person must commune with his spirit self. And when does this occur?

Here we come to the first such encounter of which we must speak. When does this occur? It happens every time we sleep in the ordinary way, roughly midway between falling asleep and waking up again. For people who are more closely connected with the life of nature, simple country folk who go to sleep when the sun sets and get up at dawn, this midway point of sleep more or less coincides with midnight. This is not so much true of people who have sundered themselves from natural connections. But that's a matter of human freedom. A person in modern life can organize his life as he likes, albeit not without this affecting his life in some way. Within certain limits he can arrange it as he wishes. But still, in the middle of a longer period of sleep, he will experience what we may call a more inward communing with the spirit self, thus with the spiritual qualities from which the spirit self will be drawn, an encounter with his genius. This encounter

with the genius occurs every night, more or less, or every time a person sleeps. And this is important for us. For the satisfying sense we can have of connection with the world of spirit depends on the continuing effect of this encounter with our genius during the night. The sense we can have in waking life of our connection with the world of spirit is an echo of this encounter with our genius. That is our first encounter with the higher world, something initially unconscious for most people today, though it will become ever more conscious the more people become aware of its after-effect as they increasingly refine the feelings in their waking consciousness by absorbing the ideas and images of spiritual science. As they do so, the soul will no longer be too coarse in nature to attend to this echo or reverberation. That is all that is needed for the soul to be fine enough in quality, to be intimate and subtle enough, to observe these after-effects. Everyone can often be aware of this encounter with their genius in some form or other. But our modern materialistic culture and environment, pervaded as it is with concepts drawn from the materialistic worldview, and especially life as lived with a materialistic outlook, is not suited to helping the soul attend to what comes about through this encounter with our genius. Simply by virtue of deepening their nature with more spiritual ideas than materialism can provide, this perception of the encounter with the genius each night will become something ever more self-evident to people.
(Berlin, 20 February 1917[20])

People today are as yet unaware of a secret of life that is intrinsically connected with humanity's present stage of evolution. In more ancient times, before the mid-fifteenth century, there was no particular need to attend to this secret. Today it is necessary. This secret of life is that, as we are presently constituted in body, soul and spirit, we look ahead each night in a particular way to the events of the coming day, although this does not mean we need necessarily have these events in our full, waking awareness. It is our angel who does. Thus what we experience in the night in union with the being we call our angel is a prefiguring view of the forthcoming day. Please do not think of this as something of mere interest to human curiosity—that would be quite wrong—but as something of practical importance. Only when we are very inwardly imbued with this outlook will we make decisions in the right way, taking thoughts over into our daily life. Imagine, say, that someone has to do something at midday. The previous night he and his angel have already been conversing about it. This has been true for people since the mid-fifteenth century. We do not need to keep this in mind, it is not a matter for curiosity. But this outlook is one that should imbue us, so that we make fruitful during the day what we weighed up with our angel the night before.

(Berlin, 13 September 1919[21])

What do the angels do in our astral body? Only by rising a little to clairvoyant perception can we discover what they do, what unfolds in our astral body. We must attain a certain degree at least of imaginative perception if we are to answer this question. And then it becomes apparent that these beings from the hierarchy of the angeloi—and in some respects every single one of the angeloi, each one of which has their own task to

perform for every human being, but also, especially their collaboration—form pictures within our astral body. Under the guidance of the Spirits of Form, they create pictures. Without rising to Imaginative cognition, we do not know that pictures are continually formed in our astral body. They arise and pass away. If such pictures were not formed, humanity could not evolve into the future in a way that accords with the intentions of the Spirits of Form. What the Spirits of Form seek to achieve with us by the end of earthly evolution must first be elaborated in pictures; and from these pictures the reality of transformed humanity will later emerge. Through the angels, the Spirits of Form are today already forming these pictures in our astral body. In the human astral body the angels form pictures to which we can attain by means of thinking developed into clairvoyance. And then one can trace and observe these images formed by the angels in our astral body. It becomes apparent when we do so that they are formed according to quite specific impulses, specific principles; in the way in which these pictures arise lie forces, in a sense, for humanity's future evolution. This sounds strange but it has to be said: if you observe the angels as they undertake this work, you find they have a very particular aim for the future shape of human society on earth. They seek to engender pictures in human astral bodies which will lead to quite particular social conditions in the human community of the future.
(Zurich, 9 October 1918[22])

In all ancient mysteries a particular teaching held true, and its content, as we become aware of it, can strike us with profound force. A pupil inducted into the ancient mysteries, gradually learning the secrets of initiation science, arrived at a certain stage of his inner development when he would describe the impressions he received as follows . . . : When I stand out in the open during the day, and direct my intuitive gaze upward, giving myself up to sense impressions, I see the sun before me. I perceive its blinding power at midday and I intuit and perceive behind this blinding strength the workings of spiritual beings of the second hierarchy in the solar realm. Before my initiation, the solar realm sank away as the sun set in the evening. The sun's rays vanished at sunset. And before my initiation I passed through the night as darkness grew around me. In the morning, at dawn, I recalled this darkness when the sun rose out of the dawn sky on its way again to the blinding brightness of midday. But having achieved initiation, this has changed: when I witness the dawn, and the sun begins to ascend into the sky again, a memory of night-time experience awakens in me. I know what I experienced during the night. I remember quite precisely how I saw a blue glimmer of light gradually spreading from sunset in the West to the East, and how, at the hour of midnight, I saw, and can now exactly recall, the sun—at a place in the sky opposite to where it stood in the radiant strength of midday—in a glow, so morally striking, behind the earth. I saw the sun at midnight.

Such initiates spoke a monologue of this kind in their meditation, and it accorded fully with the truth. To speak such words was nothing other than to bring this truth to their awareness. And when we read Jakob Boehme's words in *The Rising of Dawn*, we find there the last vestiges of a wonderful ancient teaching.

(Dornach, 27 June 1924[23])

3. Sleep as a Source of Renewal and Healing

The light of the sun
it brightens day
after dark night:
the power of the soul
has woken now
from tranquil sleep:
you, my soul
give thanks to the light
in which there shines
the power of God;
you, my soul,
do vigorous deeds.

(Handwritten note, 1919[24])

In other lectures we have mentioned the fact that sleep today is by no means unnecessary for people. It has its mighty task. During the day we wear out our physical body and etheric body. The life we lead from morning to evening involves a wearing away of both these bodies. What you feel as tiredness in the evening is nothing other than an expression of the fact that, via the astral body, perceptions of the outer world have occurred within your physical and etheric body—that feelings, impulses, suffering, pain, and all sorts of other things, have occurred within you. These things wear away the physical and etheric body during the course of the day, and in the evening we are tired because we have been working to destroy our physical and etheric body all day. When your physical and etheric body lie in bed at night, the astral body with the I is not inactive but spends the whole night sending its strength into the physical and etheric body to renew their exhausted and destroyed forces. But it could not do this if it were not taken up into a different realm as it departs from the physical and etheric body at night. Over the human realm, a spiritual realm unfolds, the realm of angels, archangels and other beings. It is like an ocean of spirit beings surrounding us, from whom we are separate during the day because we are enclosed within our bodily skin, enclosed within our sense perceptions. But at night we immerse ourselves in this ocean of spirits, and the astral body imbibes there forces which it then pours into our physical and etheric body to repair them. People today know nothing of all this. But in former times when they still possessed a dull, clairvoyant consciousness, they saw the I and the astral body emerging and being absorbed into the divine world of spirit.

(Stuttgart, 13 August 1908[25])

When a person falls asleep, the physical body and etheric body remain lying in bed, connected as they are during the day. But the astral body loosens, it and the I-body lifting as it were from the physical body. Since all sensations, ideas and so on occur within the astral body, and this is now outside the physical body, we are unconscious when asleep, for we need the physical brain as instrument to be conscious of ourselves, and without it cannot be so.

Now what does the released astral body do during the

night? The seer can observe how the astral body occupies itself in the night, performing its particular task for the sleeper. It does not hover sluggishly and inactively over us as has often been taught by theosophists, but is continually working upon the physical body. And what does it do? During the day the physical body grows tired, worn out, and this worn state, this tiredness, is reinvigorated by the astral body at night. The astral body repairs the physical body again at night and replenishes spent forces. Thus the need for sleep, and thus also the refreshing, renewing and healing nature of sleep.
(Stuttgart, 24 August 1906[26])

What does the astral body do in the night ordinarily? It is not inactive. To the seer it appears as a spiralling cloud form, from which issue currents that connect it with the prone physical body. When we are tired and fall asleep at night, what causes this tiredness? Tiredness appears because the astral body has used and worn down the physical body during waking life. But throughout the night, while we sleep, the astral body works to redress this tiredness, which is why we feel reinvigorated after a good night's sleep—and this can tell us how important really healthy sleep is for us. It renews what waking life has exhausted. The astral body remedies other disorders too during sleep, for instance illnesses of both the physical and etheric body. Besides your own personal experience, you will be aware that all good doctors regard sleep, in certain instances, as an indispensable remedy. Thus we see the importance of the alternation between sleeping and waking conditions.
(Breslau, 2 December 1908[27])

In Florence, in the Medici chapel, Michelangelo created the two Medici memorials, and four allegorical figures: Day, Night, Dawn and Dusk. People may think these are dry allegories, but if you look carefully at these four figures, you find them to be something else entirely. . . .

It is worth studying one of the figures, Night, in artistic terms, studying its gestures, the position of the resting body, the hand supporting the head, how the arm lies upon the leg. Looking at all this carefully, we can say that this is a true, outward likeness of the etheric body at its most active, when we rest at night. When we sleep, the etheric body is most active. And Michelangelo created the corresponding stance for this in his figure, Night. The way the figure lies there gives fitting expression to the active etheric body, the life body.

And if you pass on to study the figure of Day, situated on the opposite side, this is the most fitting expression for the I; and the figure of Dawn depicts the astral body, that of Evening the physical body. These are not allegories in fact but truths drawn from life itself, immortalized here with profound artistic truth. I was reluctant to acknowledge this, but the more carefully I studied these figures, the clearer it became. And now I am no longer surprised by a legend that arose in Florence at the time. It was said that Michelangelo wielded power over the figure of Night, that when he was alone in the chapel *she* got up and walked about. If *she* refers to the etheric body, this is scarcely surprising. I wished only to indicate here how clear and tangible everything becomes when we learn increasingly to consider everything from the point of view of occultism.

(Vienna, 3 November 1912[28])

Why are we not conscious when we sleep? Because the astral powers do not permit us to be, and are so strong as to stupefy us. You see, astral forces express themselves in something that entirely pervades us when asleep, that is, the burning desire to be in our body; and it is this desire that darkens our consciousness.

(Berlin, 25 April 1914[29])

If we connect what we have now said with what was stated earlier about the two poles of the human soul, we must regard the intellectual element as one pole, primarily holding sway over waking life during the day when we are awake as far as our intellect is concerned. During the day we are awake in our intellect, whereas during sleep we are awake in our will. But we are unaware of what we undertake with this will since our intellect is asleep. But into this will work what we regard as moral principles and impulses. And in fact we need our life of sleep so that the moral impulses we absorb through our thinking life can actually come to better effect. It is true to say that, as we are presently constituted in ordinary life, we can only really act adequately on the intellectual plane; we are less capable on the moral plane, for there we are dependent on help coming to us from the macrocosm.

What already lives in us can take us a good way further in our intellect, whereas the gods must come to our aid when we progress morally. That is why we succumb to sleep, so that we can immerse ourselves in the divine will, without our powerless intellect, where divine forces transform what we absorb as moral precepts into the power of the will, infusing our will with what we can otherwise only absorb in thoughts.

(Basel, 1 October 1911[30])

The preparatory exercises undertaken by the clairvoyant enquirer largely involve spiritual practices which act upon his astral body and I in such a way that, when he falls asleep, and these bodies separate from the physical and etheric body, they remain subject to the after-effect of these special preparations for clairvoyant research.

So let us consider two instances: firstly, how people ordinarily live, giving themselves up during the day to outward impressions, to all that acts upon their senses and rational thought. When they fall asleep in the evening, their astral body departs from the physical body. This astral body is then entirely given up to what the person experienced during the day, and follows not its own mobility but that of the physical body. But something different happens if, through meditation, concentration and other exercises undertaken to cultivate higher knowledge, we initiate strong effects upon our soul, thus experiencing these in our astral body and I; and if, in other words, we set aside particular times during the day when we undertake things quite differently than otherwise. At such times, instead of being involved in everything conveyed to him by his senses and reasoning, a person dwells on all he can receive and learn from worlds of spirit. Even if he practises meditation, concentration and other exercises only for a very brief time in the day, this works upon his soul so that, on emerging from the physical body at night, his astral body is affected by these practices and thus adheres to forms of elasticity different from those of the physical body. Methods to develop the capacity for clairvoyant enquiry therefore involve those who teach this capacity applying all the knowledge about such practice that people have been trying out for millennia: meditation and concentration exercises that must be undertaken in waking life to give rise to after-effects at night that reconfigure the astral body.

(Munich, 24 August 1909[31])

When we sleep, our I and astral body are immersed in the outer world, and there we unfold an intuitive activity which we must otherwise consciously develop in Intuition. But today our organization is as yet too weak to remain conscious in intuiting activity, though we do indeed live in an intuiting mode during the night. And so we can say that we develop Intuition in sleep whereas we develop logical thinking—to a certain degree only of course—in waking life. Between these two poles stand Inspiration and Imagination. When we pass over from the state of sleep into waking life, our I and astral body enter the physical body and etheric body. And what we bring with us as we do so is Inspiration, a capacity I have described in our recent lectures. So we can say that during sleep we dwell in Intuition, during waking life in logical thinking, but as we awaken we gain Inspiration, and as we fall asleep we live in Imagination.

(Dornach, 15 July 1921[32])

What people carry out in sleep, this weightless motion through an imponderable realm, can be performed spiritually in full consciousness if we have at the same time the power to

stay very still in ourselves. We can say that the sleeper follows
the impulses of moon forces, giving himself up unconsciously
to them, and performing every motion they urge him to.
Entering into conscious, exact clairvoyance, we withhold
every such movement, hold all of them back, and then these
motions metamorphose into intuitions. Thus conscious
Intuition, the highest capacity of exact clairvoyance, actually
consists in constraining what a sleeper must instinctively do,
giving himself up entirely to these powers and succumbing
fully to their sway. If we transform this, instead of being
subsumed in physical moon forces, we restrain them in
ourselves and thereby give ourselves up intuitively to the
corresponding spiritual realm, thus arriving at the faculty of
Intuition.

(Penmaenmawr, 25 August 1923[33])

Every night the human organism is actually occupied by ...
beings capable of sustaining it. Our physical and etheric
bodies lying in bed are then simultaneously pervaded by
these astral and I beings which live really in the physical body.
We can call them interlopers, though this wouldn't always be
right. We should often think of them as protective spirits
since they sustain what a person disdainfully detaches himself
from at night.

(Berlin, 4 June 1908[34])

Let's assume that someone suddenly became clairvoyant in
sleep—how will he perceive things? When we meet someone
here on the physical plane we encounter his physical form,
within which lives an I. This is not true of the world of spirit.

We must not imagine that we see a person there in the same form as on the physical plane. Here in the physical world we see things divided and separate from each other, defined by sharp outlines. It is different in the world of spirit. There life weaves and unfolds in mobile images which we can perceive to be beings, the spirits of the higher hierarchies who send their messengers, their helpers, to give the human form its right expression. These emissaries, these messengers of the Spirits of Form are still, as it were, at a childlike level, but they will develop to a higher condition to the degree to which they nurture the human I.

And another host of elemental beings, the guardians of I-being, hover around the human head. They work upon our thinking and are dispatched by the Spirits of Form and of Movement. And still other elemental beings, emissaries of the Spirits of Wisdom, act upon the human heart and bring about our blood circulation.

Then also there are elemental beings who work upon our sense of warmth. This should not be pictured in physical terms, as warmth arising from a particular heat source, for in the spiritual realm warmth is engendered in the reciprocal relationship of two beings.

Still other elemental beings work upon our sense of word, not the spoken word as one person hears another speaking, but these beings stand rather behind the various consonants and vowels that form a word, and they work upon combinations of letters and syllables.

(Berlin, 25 April 1914[35])

4. Spiritual Encounters

Only where sense knowledge ends
is the gateway found that opens
life's realities to soul existence;
the soul creates the key when she
inwardly strengthens herself
in the battle waged by cosmic powers
upon her own ground with
human forces;
when by her own might she drives away
the sleep that at the limits of the senses
wraps powers of knowledge
in spiritual night.

(Vienna 6 May 1915[36])

What lives inside minerals becomes very clear to someone who can enter consciously into this world which is otherwise inhabited in the deepest sleep. And when we dwell in a world like that within minerals it seems that we are inhabiting the stone rather than observing it from without. You will recognize from what I am saying something I sought to express in a certain passage in my book *Theosophy*. In this account of spirit land, certainly, you discover this reversal. By living into this reversal we find our way into a world where we can participate not only in the deeds of the higher hierarchies but in their very beings, coming to know these beings as we can here acquaint ourselves with people's qualities of soul in the physical world. We are then no longer in the inspired world but in that of Intuition. We now give ourselves up not only to the deeds, the spirit deeds of these spirit beings, but to these beings themselves.

But then we are also in the world in which karma becomes actuality for us. In this third state of sleep, if we could suddenly become conscious within it, we would perceive our karma. We would perceive how our past lives play into our present life on earth. We experience our karma in deep sleep, and we also carry the fruits of this experience back into our physical body. But the physical body is not suited to perceiving such a thing. Initially it has no organs for it. Just as our eyes are adapted to seeing externally, and our ears to hearing external sounds, so we need to develop organs of inner perception.

(Bern, 21 March 1922[37])

Various other things can tell us how we are karmically connected with someone else. Some of you will have realized that there are people in your life you don't dream about. You might live a long time with them but they never figure in your dreams. Then there are others you meet whom you keep dreaming about, who won't stay out of your dreams. Hardly have you met them than you're dreaming about them repeatedly.

Dreams draw on things in the subconscious. People we dream about the moment we meet them are ones we are karmically connected with. People we can't dream about make only a passing impression on our senses, and we meet them without any prior karmic connection.

What lives in the depths of our will is like a waking dream. And for the initiate this waking dream becomes the full content of consciousness. This is why he hears someone karmically connected with him speaking from within him. Naturally he always remains sensible: he doesn't go around and, as an initiate, speak out of all sorts of others who speak to him. But in some circumstances he does accustom himself, even if others are not physically present, to really and tangibly addressing those karmically connected with him, who speak out of him, as in a conversation; and this gives rise to things that also have real significance.

(Dornach, 27 January 1924[38])

Sleep unites us with the world of spirit. It sends us over into that world. And people should at least develop something they could put in words like these: 'I fall asleep. Until I awaken my soul will be in the spiritual world, where it will meet the guiding power and being of my earthly life, who lives in the world of spirit, who hovers around my head; it will meet my genius. And on awakening I will have had this encounter. The wings of my genius will have caressed my soul.'

A very great deal depends on whether or not we bring this kind of feeling alive in us when we reflect on our relationship with sleep: the capacity to overcome materialistic life depends on it. Overcoming materialistic life can only happen if we kindle subtle feelings, though ones that correspond to the spiritual world. Only by soliciting such feelings will our life in sleep become so keen, our contact with the world of spirit so strong, that gradually our waking life also can gain strength from this, so that we not only have the world of senses around us but the spiritual world—which is after all the real, the truly real world.

(Berlin, 20 February 1917[39])

Generally people are protected by what we call the Guardian of the Threshold from perceiving the world of spirit surrounding them at night. But when we have passed through the gate of death, after the first few days when we lay aside the etheric body, we enter a retrospective existence between death and rebirth: starting with the day of our death we pass backward to the day before and so on, once again reviewing our life backward from death to birth. Yet we do not re-experience our waking days but our nights, and therefore the time we spend in this backward review takes roughly a third of the life we lived. For someone who dies at the age of 60, this retrospective review will take around twenty years. This period of life after death happens three times faster than our life on earth did. And during this time we are gazing on our nightly experiences in which, albeit unconsciously, images were evoked that are in a way negative reflections of the life we led.

If we were not protected by the Guardian of the Threshold, our experience every night would be one we could not endure, with consequences like those I just described: it would be as if we had done something wicked to someone else and must inhabit this other person, inhabit what he experiences and feels through the evil done to him. During sleep we do truly inhabit the being on whom we have inflicted one thing or another, but for the reason I stated we do not become aware of this during sleep. After death, though, we do experience it during the period I described, in a very acute way indeed. Then we live back through our life on earth and have compensatory experiences of what we either did or omitted to do. *(Stuttgart, 1 June 1924[40])*

It cannot but fill us with the greatest humility and amazement to see how whole hosts of elemental beings are at work upon the wonderful temple of the human body.

Enter into this mood in earnest meditation: how countless elemental beings build the glorious temple that is to form the habitation of the human I!

But now let us ask why it is that we do not see these elemental beings at work in this way. It is because, as we waken from sleep, the Guardian of the Threshold veils the worlds of spirit from view. Waking up actually means nothing other than to scare away these elemental beings from their place of work. And the moment we regain our waking awareness, Ahriman ensures that the world of spirit is concealed: he paints before our eyes the tableau of the sense world; and in giving ourselves to Maya, the great illusionist, souls or beings who work upon the human being's spiritual organization become invisible to our gaze.

What we recognize as physical body is all the work of Ahriman. By contrast what we experience as our inner life in merely physical life must be seen as the work of Lucifer. He fills our soul with such pride and bedazzlement that we acquire false ideas and feelings about the world of spirit. Ex Deo nascimur, In * morimur, Per Spiritum Sanctum reviscimus. *(Berlin, 25 April 1914[41])*

When a person falls into deep, dreamless sleep which, though, through the gift of Inspiration, is no longer dreamless for him but can be seen and perceived, then these beings, the undines, rise up before his spiritual vision out of the astral ocean in which in a sense the gnomes interred him as he fell asleep; they become visible in deep sleep. Sleep extinguishes our usual awareness. But awareness illumined in sleep has this wonderful world of fluid growth, whose content is a fluid uprush in which these undines pass through every possible kind of metamorphosis. Just as we have before us in waking consciousness entities with fixed and delineated contours, the night's illumined consciousness would present these continually transforming beings rising and sinking in wave-like motion. The whole of our deep sleep is really pervaded by a moving sea of living beings around us, a moving ocean of undines. . . .

After we have slept all night, having around us this astral sea of undines in the most diverse configurations, and then awaken with a wakening dream, this would—if we saw the dream unmasked and not overlaid by reminiscences of our life or by emblems of our inner organs—appear to us as the world of sylphs. Yet these sylphs would assume curious form for us: as if the sun sought to send us something that acts on us in a difficult way, in a sense sending us into a spiritual slumber . . . . Nevertheless, if we saw our waking dream unmasked, we would see in it something like the flitting in of light, of beings of light. And we would experience this as unpleasant also because the limbs of these sylphs would be spinning a floating tangle around us. We would feel the light was attacking us from all sides, as if light were something that beset us, and to which we are extraordinarily sensitive. We might also now and then experience this as the caress of light. But with all these things I only want to give you a subtle sense of how the sustaining fingers of this light approach us and touch us in the form of sylphs.

(Dornach, 3 November 1923[42])

Without being a spiritual scientist yourself, you can still create a real connection with a dead person. However, you will in a sense have to wait for the right moment to send the dead soul something that really reaches him. Usually for someone who isn't a conscious initiate, and does not have a conscious connection with the world of spirit, the moment of particular importance for creating this relationship will be that of falling asleep. The moment when you pass from waking life into sleep is also usually when anything you have sent in the dead person's direction during the day, as I have described this, will make its way to them. The path that conducts you yourself into the world of spirit as you fall sleep also conducts what you have sent upward to the dead soul, into the realm of the dead. For this reason you must be cautious when interpreting dreams, which are very often only reminiscences, memories of waking life, though they need not necessarily be. They can certainly mirror realities. And especially—not always but very often—the dreams where you dream of a dead person can come from your connection with the actual soul of the dead person. But it would be wrong to think, as people often do, that what appears to them in dream, what the dead person communicates to them, is to be taken at face value as direct reality. No. In fact, what you wanted to communicate to the dead person when you fell asleep is absorbed by them, and what appears in a dream is the way, or the fact, that they absorb it. Thus when a dead person communicates something to you in a dream, this should tell you that you have been able to communicate with them. Rather than thinking that the dead person has appeared to you in a dream and told you a particular thing, it is much more probable that dreaming of them is an expression of the fact that what you wanted to say to them did actually reach them, and that they are showing you this as you dream of them.

The moment of awakening is of particular importance for receiving an actual response from the dead person. It is at this moment, when we awaken, that what the dead have to communicate to us, as we say, is carried back from realms of spirit. This rises from the depths of our own soul. People commonly do not attend much to what surfaces in them from the depths of their own soul. In our time people generally don't have much sense for attending to what rises from the depths of their souls. They prefer to receive impressions from without, only wish to assimilate the outer world, and by so doing like to numb themselves to what rises from deep within. But when a person does notice that a thought or idea has risen from deep in his soul he thinks he is inspired, and this is likely to flatter his vanity. Such things may be our own inspiration, but mostly these sudden brainwaves are the answer given us by the dead, for the dead certainly live with us. Thus what apparently comes from within you is actually what the dead are saying. And it is important to interpret such things in the right way. I have often detailed the ways in

which we can communicate with the dead, such as reading aloud to them and so forth. The more we live in these things vividly, pictorially and with keen feeling, the more significantly will our connection with the dead person become.
(Hamburg, 30 June 1918[43])

5. The Starry Firmament

My head bears
the existence of resting stars,
my breast harbours
the life of wandering planets,
my body takes being
in the being of the elements.
This am I.

(For Walter Johannes Stein, April 1924[44])

Now imagine you are standing in a field on a clear, star-bright night, and can survey the great expanse of the starry heavens above you. Gazing at this whole expanse, you can see areas denser with stars and therefore appearing almost misty, and other areas of the heavens where the stars are more isolated from each other, forming the patterns of the constellations and so on. If you gaze at this sight with a merely intellectual mode of observation, that of human reason, you get nowhere to start with. But you feel things differently if you ponder this starry firmament with your whole being. Nowadays we have lost this feeling capacity but it can be reacquired. And then we will have a different feeling about areas of the heavens where the stars are so close together that they appear like mist, from areas where the constellations are found. We have a different feeling about the place in the sky where, say, the moon is shining, and a night without a moon will give us a different feeling again, as will the time of new moon and so on. And just as we can feel our way specifically into the human organism to experience the three dimensions, where space acquires a tangible quality, a connection with us, so we can acquire a perception of the cosmos, of the whole compass of the heavens. To arrive at an experience such as that of three dimensions we need not only look inside ourselves but can now also look out into far breadths around us. And if we learn how to attend to this expanse, passing on from the usual perception which is sufficient for geometry to one we need for these breadths, we gain a form of perception which I referred to yesterday and the day before as imaginative cognition, a faculty whose development I will be speaking about.

If you were simply to note what you see in the breadths of the cosmos, you would get nowhere. Merely depicting and recording the starry sky as modern astronomers do, leads to nothing. But if you stand before this cosmos with your full humanity and understanding, then images form within the soul of these denser configurations of stars, such as those you can see on old star-charts from a time when people still formed imaginations through a capacity for ancient, instinctive clairvoyance. And then you develop an Imagination of the whole cosmos. You acquire the counterpart to what I described yesterday as the foundations within human nature of the three geometrical dimensions of space. You acquire something that can be configured in infinite ways.
(The Hague, 9 April 1922[45])

As we descend from cosmic, spiritual breadths to an earthly existence, we always approach this new life from a particular star. We can trace this direction and it is not inappropriate, but on the contrary very precise, to say that each person does have their own star. A particular star, a fixed star, is the human being's spiritual home.

If we transpose what is after all experienced outside of time and space between death and rebirth into its spatial image, then we have to say that each person has his star, which determines what he elaborates between death and rebirth, and he approaches a new life from the direction of a particular star.

(Dornach, 6 July 1924[46])

Certainly there are still people who sometimes go out on bright, starry nights and enjoy the whole glory and magnificence of the sparkling firmament, but there are ever fewer of them, and they are increasingly outnumbered by those who cannot even tell a planet from a star. But that's not the most important thing. Even when people go out and look up at the star-bright sky, they can see stars only in an external way, as physical objects. It was not so in olden times; nor was it so for souls who are now here and in ancient times were incarnated in other bodies. The same souls who nowadays see stars only as physical objects once looked up to the starry heavens and saw not so much the stars' physical light but what is spiritually connected with the stars. And spiritual beings are connected with all the stars.

(Linz, 26 January 1913[47])

Let us consider times when people still scarcely sought the desired content of their spiritual and cultural life on the earth, but turned away from the earth to the cosmos to find the deepest content which their sensibility required. Let us consider times when people had clairvoyant capacities which they brought to bear on the positions of the fixed stars, and the movements of the planets, regarding everything on earth as a reflection of what unfolds in the earth's cosmic surroundings. We need only think of the ancient Egyptians and how they regarded the life-giving Nile in relation to the appearance of the star Sirius, in relation to the rising of a particular star. They could only fathom what the Nile meant for their lives by seeing this as an outcome of the cosmos, and observing, as they gazed up at the heavens, how the position of a particular star related to another. The way in which one star was connected with another in the great expanse of the cosmos was reflected for them in earthly conditions, for instance in the Nile's fluctuations.

This is just one example, for in general they regarded anything that happened anywhere on earth as a reflection of secrets observed in the starry heavens. And we must realize that in those far-off times, people saw quite different things in the starry sky than whatever is computed and calculated today in mechanical or chemical terms. But today I'd like to look quite particularly at how people of those times, as they received the spiritual content for their soul, their sensibility, gave expression to this in, let us say, poetic form.

This was a time when art forms other than poetry were less developed. They did exist but in more rudimentary form, and this was because a person of those long-gone times knew that words, which he drew from the inmost mystery of his organization, could bring something supersensible to expression, that speech could best express what manifests supersensibly through the constellations and movements of the stars. This was a better vehicle than any other materials used in art, which inevitably had to be taken directly from the earth's substance. The word originates in our spiritual aspect—that is what people felt in olden times. And for this reason it best corresponded to what manifests from cosmic breadths as a descending impulse. It was in poetry, first and foremost, as an offspring not of imagination alone but of spiritual vision, that people learned what subsequently flowed into the other arts. Poetry, finding its expression in words, was certainly felt to be the point of departure for establishing a relationship and soul communion with super-terrestrial reality.

The mood of poetry really equated with this raising of oneself to soul communion with the super-terrestrial realm. Through this soul communion people felt how the thought, which they did not yet sunder from things, comes to pictorial expression in the human head, in the firmament-like dome of the upper head, and itself embodies a spiritual firmament, a spiritual dome of the heavens. The thoughts people experienced transposed them into the entirety of the cosmos. Separate thoughts were expressed through the way in which the stars related to each other, circling and passing one another. In those ancient times, a person did not merely think out of his own inner impetus. This only came about in the greater freedom of later times. Back then people experienced every motion of thought as the after-image of a movement in the cosmos: every figure or form of thought was an after-image of a heavenly constellation. When people

thought, they felt themselves transposed into the stars; and
for this reason it was not the sunlight of daytime that seemed
to point them toward wisdom. It blinded them, rather, to
what really guided and oriented their thoughts. They saw the
sun, it is true, as a luminous source, but only in terms of the
moon shining the sun's light through the world of stars.
During the day, people said—and this was certainly part of
ancient mystery wisdom—that they saw the light with their
physical body, but at night they saw this sunlight held in the
moon's silver goblet. The moon was the silver goblet that
held sunlight at night. And this night-time sunlight, vesseled
in the silver moon, was an elixir for the soul, a soma drink.
Spiritualized by this soma elixir, the soul could comprehend
thoughts which were, really, the fruit and reflection of the
starry heavens.

(Dornach, 8 June 1923[48])

As a thinker, a person felt as if the power of his thinking did
not inhabit his earthbound organism but as if it lived where
the stars circle and form the constellations. A person felt as if
his soul were poured out into the whole world. And he would
not have sought logical laws if he had been investigating the
connections or divisions of thoughts but would have traced
the paths of the stars, the zodiac images in the nightly firmament if he had wished to know how thoughts inter-
connect, how they detach from each other. In the heavens he
sought the laws and images for his thinking.

And then, when he considered his feeling, when he
became aware of his feeling, this was not the abstract kind of
thinking we mean in our abstract times, but a tangible feeling

that united what we refer to as feeling today in the abstract with an inner experience of breathing, of blood circulation, with the whole lively pulse of activity within the human body. In the connection between blood circulation and breathing he experienced the weaving of the soul element in him. And he did not feel himself solely upon the physical earth either but in the realm of the planets. Instead of picturing millions of little blood corpuscles circulating in the human organism, he felt Mercury and Mars interweaving with sun and moon. He felt his sensibility poured out into the cosmos, the difference between thinking and feeling here being that in his thoughts he dwelt more with the fixed stars and their images, and in feeling more in the planetary realm, the motions of the planets. Only in his will did he feel himself to be upon the earth. In their sense that earthly reality was a reflection of the cosmos, people told themselves that when the forces of Jupiter, of the moon, of Venus or the sun infused the earth, penetrating the ground's elements of mineral, water, air, then from these solid, fluid, gaseous elements, will impulses pervaded them like the thought impulses from the fixed stars, and the feeling impulses from the motions of the planets.

Through such feelings people at that time were still able to carry themselves back to a period when the earliest form of art first originated in humanity. What kind of art was this? Nothing other than human language itself. Nowadays people have little sense of speech and language as the primordial, originating art, for our language now is bound to material, earthly things. Our language no longer bears its original character when people felt transported into the zodiac, and incorporated into themselves the twelve consonants through their sense of the zodiac pictures, and the vowels in their sense of the movement of the planets through these zodiac constellations. When, rather than expressing earthly experience, they sought to express in speech what the soul felt to be its far flight from the earth out into the cosmos, their language was raised into ancient poetry. Then, in language, a reflection arose in them of what they experienced in soul communion with the cosmos. All ancient poetry really originated from this experience of the soul communing with the spiritual cosmos. The last vestiges of such poetry are found for instance in the Vedas and, though by then already in far more abstract form, in the Edda. These were still replications of something that had arisen in far greater glory, far greater nobility and majesty in primordial times, as languages themselves were configured, when people had been able to feel their soul life in these languages in inward communion with the cosmic movements.

What remains in modern poetry of those primordial times? Poetry would not be poetry—and in our era of course much of it isn't—if it didn't retain something at least of that communing life of the earthly human being with the cosmos. *(Dornach, 8 June 1923[49])*

These people [in ancient times] had living perception of the spiritual beings of the elements. In those days their senses were usually not configured to see only stars as night fell, but they saw, rather, imaginations, saw the spiritual realities living in the starry heavens. This is why I have often pointed out that the curious figures to be found on ancient star charts were not, as modern science assumes, the result of random fantasy, but came from direct vision. People really saw these things.

These ancient people therefore created and counselled out of their direct vision, and established social co-existence accordingly.

(Berlin, 19 June 1917[50])

In the same way that ... during the daytime we are immersed in our blood circulation, so in the soul life of the night we are immersed in a replication of the planetary motions of our solar system. In the day we say that the white and red blood corpuscles are circulating in us, that the power of respiration is enlivening us. For the night, by contrast, we must say that a replica of the motions of Mercury, of Venus, of Jupiter circulate in us. During sleep, our soul life is a kind of small planetary cosmos. Emerging from the personal, human realm, our life becomes cosmic from the moment we fall asleep to that of re-awakening. And inspired knowledge can then discover how, when we are tired in the evening, the forces which kept our blood pulsing during the day can maintain vitality through the night by their own capacity of persistence, but that in order to be turned again into the soul life of day, these forces require the fresh impulse that comes from the experience of a replica of the planetary cosmos during the night. As we awaken, an after-effect of our experience of this replica of the planetary motions during sleep is implanted or infused into us, and this is what connects the cosmos to our individual life. When we wake up in the morning, the forces we need could not properly stream in to us in the right way, to render us properly conscious, if we did not have this after-effect of nightly experiences.

(Stuttgart, 9 October 1922[51])

Our experience of the fixed stars—which can arise in some people half an hour after falling asleep, in others after a longer period, and in still others very soon after falling asleep—is one of being within all twelve constellations.[52] These experiences of the fixed stars are extraordinarily complex.

It seems to me that a globe-trotter who had journeyed to all the major regions of the earth would not have had the totality of experiences vouchsafed to your solar eye every night from a single constellation of the zodiac! In ancient times people found this all relatively less confusing since they still possessed powers of dreamlike seership and perceived much of what I am now relating with a dreamlike awareness. Today it is scarcely possible for someone to reach any degree of clarity with his solar eye about what he experiences during the night in twelvefold complexity—though he must, even if this is forgotten again in the daytime—unless he has incorporated into his sensibility what the Christ sought to become through the Mystery of Golgotha. Simply to have felt what it signifies for earthly life that Christ underwent the Mystery of Golgotha, simply to have given a little thought to Christ in ordinary life, tinges the astral body, via the physical and etheric body, in such a way that Christ becomes our guide through the zodiac during the hours of sleep.

A person will feel that he might inevitably founder in the numerous stars and their occurrences, but if he can look back on thoughts, feelings and will impulses with which he turned toward Christ during the day, then a kind of guide arises from him in the Christ, ordering the confusing and complex occurrences in this sphere. . . .

Much of the state of being that a person who seeks a degree of self-knowledge will find within him is a very dull echo of this experience of Christ as our guide through Aries, Taurus, Gemini and so on, and his explanations to us of the world during the night so that we gain strength again for daily life. In this sphere we experience nothing less than Christ as our guide through the confusing occurrences of the zodiac: of this guiding figure leading us from constellation to constellation so that we can assimilate in an ordered fashion forces that we need again for our waking life.

(London, 30 August 1922[53])

People before the Mystery of Golgotha—and we were all in this situation in previous lives, we ourselves are these people we're talking about—used to sink into sleep and experience the anxiety I described; but Christ at that time was always present as an after-image from the world of stars in the same way as the other after-images of stars. And whenever they slept, Christ approached them with such good help, dispersing and driving away their fears. In ancient times, in their instinctive clairvoyance, people also still possessed a kind of memory when they woke up again, a kind of dreamlike memory of Christ having been with them as they slept. They called him the sun spirit. These people living before the time of the Mystery of Golgotha acknowledged the great sun spirit as the great guide and helper of humanity, who came to them each night in sleep to take away their fears of being fragmented, splintered apart into the world. Christ appeared to them as the spirit who consolidated them inwardly and gave them stability.

(Kristiania [Oslo], 18 May 1923[54])

6. Sacred and Holy Nights

Christmas Mood

As though released from a spell I feel
the spirit child in the lap of the soul:
in heart's bright light the holy Word of worlds
has now engendered hope's heavenly fruit
which grows rejoicing into the wide cosmos
out of my being's ground of God.

(Soul Calendar, 1912/13[55])

In the Christmas night, a person can picture how, in his physical, etheric and astral body, he is related to the threefold cosmos: its etheric appearing so majestically, but also magically before him in the blue of the night heavens, the astral nature of the cosmos appearing to him in the influx of the light of stars. In the holiness of these surroundings, and its relation to what is earthly, he can feel how his I-being is transposed into the spatial realm. And then he may gaze upon the Christmas mystery, the newborn child, the representative of humanity on earth born into these spatial conditions and, as a child, embarking on them. And in perceiving the Christmas thought in its wealth and majesty as he contemplates the child born at Christmas, he can say: Ex Deo nascimur—I was born out of the divine that infuses and pervades space.

But having felt this fully, having imbued himself with this, he can recollect the truth which anthroposophy teaches him about the meaning and purpose of the earth. This child whom we contemplate is of course the outward mantle of what has been born into space. And what is he born from, so as to be born into space? In the terms of our deliberations today, this can only be time. He is born out of time.

And as we trace the life of this child, seeing how the being of Christ indwells and spiritualizes him, we realize that this Christ being comes from the sun. And gazing up to the sun we can say that we discern, in its light, time hidden from space. Time indwells the sun's interior. And from this time that weaves within the sun, Christ entered spatial conditions upon earth. So what do we have in the Christ on earth? We have what connects, unites with earth from outside space, something that comes from without.

Now consider how our picture and idea of the universe is altered from our usual ideas of it if we really take this contemplation seriously! In the universe we have the sun with everything that appears part of it in the cosmos, all that is enclosed in the blue of the sky, the world of stars. There we also have the earth with humanity. But as we look up from the earth to the sun, we are gazing also into the flow of time.

Something very significant follows from this: that we only look up rightly at the sun if, in the spirit, say, we forget space and heed only time. As such, the sun does not only emanate light but also space itself. And when we look into the sun, we are looking away from the realm of space. That is why the sun is this unique star: because, through it, we look away from space. But it is from this realm outside space that Christ came to humankind. When Christ founded Christianity on earth, human beings had been all too long merely in the Ex Deo nascimur, had formed an affinity with it and had lost time altogether. They had become nothing but beings of space.

With our modern consciousness and culture we find it so hard to understand old traditions, since these invariably reckon with space, really, and not with the element of time: they regard time, temporality, only as an appendage to the spatial realm.

Then came Christ, bringing us the element of time again. And as human hearts, human souls, human spirits, unite with the Christ, they regain the stream of time from eternity to eternity. What else can we human beings do when we die and, in other words, depart this world of space, than cling again to what gives us time back, since, at the era of Golgotha, humanity had become beings of space to such a degree that they had lost time! Christ brought time back to us again. *(Dornach, 4 June 1924[56])*

If, on this day that should be consecrated and dedicated to a recollection of the Christ impulse, we can feel that something is kindled in our hearts throughout the year through our earnest endeavours in spiritual science, then our hearts will feel that these places where we gather are cribs, and these candles here are symbols! These cribs, by virtue of the sacred mood contained here, and these candles by virtue of their symbolic gleam, contain what should be prepared by both Christmas and Easter as a great era for humanity: the resurrection of the holiest spirit, of truly spiritual life!

Let us try to feel this: that our auditoria become cribs at

Christmas, places where, secluded from the outer world, something magnificent is being prepared. Let us learn to feel that if we learn diligently all year then our insight, the wisdom we have earned, can culminate on this Christmas Eve in fiery feelings leaping from the fuel we gather all year by immersing ourselves in great teachings. And let us feel that in doing so we cultivate remembrance of the greatest impulse in humanity's evolution, that the belief can live here among us that the sacred flame and hopeful beam originally kindled in the small confines of a crib will shine out into humanity. Then it will be strong enough, powerful enough to penetrate even the most obdurate, prosaic nature of life, firing, warming and illumining it. And then we can feel the Christmas mood here to be one of hope for that great Easter mood of the world, which will give expression to the living spirit needed by a new humanity.

We best celebrate Christmas within our soul if we fill the coming days with this mood: fill it so that with our Christmas we are spiritually preparing the Easter of humanity, the resurrection of spiritual life. Yes indeed, our places of work should become cribs at Christmastide. The child of light should be born, kindled throughout the year by our immersion in spiritual-scientific wisdom. Christ must be born in the human soul within our places of study and work so that spiritual life can be reborn at the great Eastertide of humanity. This humanity must feel resurrected by spirituality through the Christmas mood that we send streaming from our centres to the universal humanity of today and the future.

(Berlin, 22 December 1910[57])

In certain medieval periods people could feel a mood that arose as the nights grew darker in autumn and Christmas approached. Their inner experiences resonated with all that lives in outward nature, with the snow, the falling snowflakes, icicles on the trees. Only at this time of year did they feel a very special mood, which strengthened their souls and imbued them with a healing virtue for the whole year. This really did renew the soul, it was a real power. Decades ago one might still encounter the last vestiges of such feelings. I can tell you, and witnessed it myself in completely mundane ways, that back then you could find the most wayward lads, real good-for-nothings who would not dare to be impious as the days grew shorter. Those who always got into brawls were suddenly mischievous no longer, and those who rarely brawled stopped doing so altogether around Christmas time. A real power lived in people's souls. For a few weeks around Christmas this whole world of feeling held sway.

And what was it really that people were feeling? Condensed into feeling was a sense of our descent from divine, spiritual heights to the deepest nadir of the physical plane; a receiving of the Christ impulse, a turnabout of the human being's path, and our rise again to divine, spiritual heights. This feeling arose from everything connected with the Christ event.

(Stuttgart, 27 December 1910[58])

Oh it has to be said that a profound feeling awakens in our soul when, compressed into the one night from 24 to 25 December, we find in our reflections, our feeling reflections, what humanity received through the luciferic powers in the journey from Adam and Eve through to the birth of Christ in Jesus. If we can feel this, then we do adequately feel the significance of this festival, and what could be set before humanity through it.

When people use this occasion, this waymarker in time, as meditative contemplation, then it does seem possible for humanity to become aware of its pure origins in the cosmic powers of the universe. Raising its gaze to the cosmic powers of the universe, and delving through Theosophia, through real spiritual wisdom, a little way into the secrets of the universe, humanity can become ripe again to comprehend a higher level of the festival of the birth of Jesus in the way the gnostics comprehended it—the festival that should by rights be celebrated on 6 January: that of the birth of Christ within the body of Jesus of Nazareth. But, as if to enable us to immerse ourselves in the twelve universal powers of the cosmos, the twelve holy nights intervene between the Christmas festival and the one that ought to be celebrated on 6 January, and nowadays is the festival of the Three Kings.

Without scholars so far recognizing it, these twelve holy nights stand here again as if ordained by the soul depths of humanity's hidden wisdom. It is as if they wished to tell us that we should experience the full profundity of the Christ festival but then, during the twelve holy nights, immerse ourselves in the holiest secrets of the cosmos—that is, in the realm of the universe from which Christ descended to earth. For only if humanity will let itself be inspired by the thought of the holy child as the human being's divine origin, by the wisdom that penetrates the twelve powers, the twelve holy powers of the universe symbolically represented in the twelve signs of the zodiac, but truly embodying spiritual wisdom, will a humanity of the future find the Inspiration that can come to us from the festival of Jesus' birth. Only when humanity immerses itself in true spiritual wisdom and learns to perceive the unfolding course of time in the great cosmos and each individual human being, only then, made fruitful by spiritual science, will we find the most assured, most hopeful idea of the future.

And so we should let the Christmas festival work upon our soul as a festival of Inspiration, as one that summons before us so wonderfully the thought of the human being's source and origin in the holy, divine child. The light that in the holy night of Christmas Eve shines forth to us as the originating symbol of the light in humanity, symbolized in more recent times by the candles on the Christmas tree, is at the same time, if rightly understood, the light that can best strengthen our soul in its quest for true, authentic universal peace, true, authentic universal blessedness, true, authentic universal hope.

May we let such thoughts of past deeds, of the root we grow from, strengthen us for what we always need in the way of future impulses: Christmas thoughts, recollections of the origin of humanity, thoughts which that root sustains so that we can flourish and grow into the healthiest soul plant, into an authentic human future.

(Berlin, 21 December 1911[59]*)*

The period of the Christmas festival embodies earth's inward holding of breath, when it has fully absorbed soul and spirit. Deep in the earth's interior rests everything which the earth unfolded during summer so that the cosmos might quicken it. Everything that opened itself and gave itself up to cosmic forces during summer, has now been sucked in by the earth and at Christmastide rests in the earth's depths. As human beings we do not of course live in the depths of the earth but we live physically on its surface. Nor do our spirit and soul live in the bowels of the earth either, but really dwell in the earth's wider surroundings. Soul-spiritually we also live in the atmosphere that encircles the earth.

For this reason all esoteric learning has always acknowledged that the essence of the earth at the winter solstice, at Christmas, is something initially concealed, that cannot be discerned by ordinary human powers of cognition, that belongs in the realm of esoteric mysteries. And in all more ancient times when something like our Christmas festival was celebrated, it was held that what happens with the earth at that time of year could only be understood through initiation into mystery knowledge, into what was known in ancient Greece as the chthonic mysteries. Through such initiation into the mysteries, a person would estrange himself in a sense from the earth, where he lived with his ordinary awareness, immersing himself in something he could not physically immerse himself in: he would submerse himself in the soul-spiritual realm, coming to know what the earth becomes at midwinter by breathing in and absorbing its spirit and soul. (*Dornach, 1 April 1923*[60])

The Christmas festival hearkens back to the night of initiation held in the great mysteries. At such events the initiator enabled the higher man to be reborn within those who had undergone sufficient preparation for this; or, to use more common parlance today, within whom the living Christ was born. . . .

This preparation of mystery pupils for awakening involved first teaching them the significance of this awakening for the greater universe. Only then were the final rites for awakening undertaken, at a time when the darkness is greatest, when the outer sun stands lowest in the sky: at Christmastide. Those familiar with spiritual realities know that this is when cosmic space is pervaded by forces favourable to such awakening. During preparation the pupil was told that, if he really wished to gain knowledge, he would need to survey not only what has occurred on earth for millennia past but also the whole of humanity's evolution. He must learn too that the great festivals of the year had been ordained by leading individuals, and that they must be dedicated to the great, eternal truths and human acknowledgement of them. . . .

And today let us share in the experience of what occurred at midnight in the lesser mysteries. This was the same everywhere: in the Egyptian mysteries, in those at Eleusis, in Asia Minor, in the mysteries of Babylonia and Chaldea, in Persian Mithras worship and in the Brahma mysteries in India. Everywhere pupils of these mystery schools had the same experience at midnight on the night we now call Christmas Eve. They gathered in good time in the early evening, and had to ponder in quiet reflection on the significance of this most important event. They sat in deep silence in the dark together. And when midnight approached, they had been sitting there for hours already. Thoughts of eternity unfolded within them. And then, toward midnight, mysterious tones could be heard filling the room, surging and fading. Hearing these tones, the pupils knew them to be the music of the spheres. Profound, sacred reverence filled their hearts. And then a weak light began to glimmer, issuing from a faintly illumined disc. Those who saw this knew that the disc represented the earth. The illumined disc now grows ever darker until finally it is completely black, while at the same time light brightens in the room. Seeing this, they knew that the sun, which otherwise illumines the earth, has become hidden from view; the earth can no longer perceive the sun. Then rainbow colours begin to spread outward from the earth disc, in circle after circle. Seeing this, they knew it to be the iris. At midnight, in place of the black sphere of the earth, there rose a luminous violet-red sphere on which a word was inscribed. The word differed according to different cultures where this mystery was enacted. In our modern language it would be 'Christos'. Seeing this, the pupils knew it to be the sun. It appeared to them at midnight, when the rest of the world dwells in deepest darkness. And the pupils were taught that they had now experienced in images what is called in the mysteries 'seeing the sun at midnight'.

Someone who has been truly initiated really does learn to see the sun at midnight, for the material world has been extinguished in him. Only the sun of spirit lives within him, and outshines all the darkness of matter.

This is the most blessed moment in humanity's evolution: when a person finds that he is living in eternal light and released from darkness. It is this moment that was pictorially conveyed as I have described, year after year in the mysteries, at midnight on Christmas Eve.

(Berlin, 17 December 1906[61])

But if you are connected with the spirit of the earth, with what lives spiritually within the earth, you awaken to your inwardness; that is, like Olaf Åsteson, you fall asleep outwardly, preferably at the Christmas period, during the thirteen nights. This is also an esoteric reality, signifying for occultism precisely the same as, say, the reality of the sun's outward position signifies for materialistic science. Of course, scientists will think it self-evident to describe the passage of the sun in summer and winter in purely external, astronomical terms, and will regard as idiocy the esoteric reality that the spiritual position of the sun is most intense in winter time, and that therefore conditions then are most favourable for someone who seeks a deepening of soul connected with the spirit of the earth and all spiritual truth. Someone seeking such deepening will find that he best experiences this in the thirteen days of Christmas: that at this period, without us noticing it, experiences rise up within. But it is also true to say that in modern times people are more emancipated from outward conditions so that occult experiences can arise at any time. But in so far as outward things do still affect us, the time between Christmas and New year is the most important period of the year for these things.

(Berlin, 7 January 1913[62])

At Christmas time the gods gaze in upon the earth and discern all that lives in human beings and departs from them with their I and astral nature. We really should ponder the following picture which describes a reality: that in winter the earth's windows open and the angels and archangels behold how people are on earth.

Here on earth, in modern culture, we have gradually accustomed ourselves to accepting that our knowledge of things must inevitably be couched in sober and prosaic ways, that it is unpoetic. Higher beings always remain poets, and it is therefore always wrong to describe their nature in sober, prosaic, physical words. Instead, we must always reach for words such as the ones I just used when I said that in winter the earth's windows open and the angels and archangels gaze through to see what human beings are doing all year. The beings of the higher hierarchies, even when they think, are poets and artists. The logical thinking we tend to engage in and elaborate is only an outcome of the earth's gravity— which is not to say of course that it isn't very valuable on earth.

Now for these angelic beings, the essential thing living in human beings is really the sensibility that comes to expression in their conduct. Angels gazing through the Christmas windows are not interested in the elaborate thoughts of university professors, or so much in our thoughts in general. What is happening in human feelings, in human soul and sensibility, is connected with this seasonal cycle of the sun and its cosmic significance. Whether we are stupid or clever on earth is not of much concern before the gaze of divine, spiritual worlds, but only whether we are good people or bad, people of keen sensitivity or egotists. It is this that is conveyed to cosmic worlds through the seasons' cyclical dynamic.

(Dornach, 1 December 1922[63]*)*

Winter solstice

See the sun
at deep midnight,
use stones to build
in the lifeless ground.

So find in decline
and in death's night
creation's new beginning,
morning's fresh power.

Let the heights reveal
the eternal word of gods;
the depths sustain and nurture
the stronghold of peace.

Living in darkness
engender a sun;
weaving in substance,
see spirit's bliss.

(Berlin, 17 December 1906[64])

7. Meditations as Prelude and Epilogue to the Night

Like stars the god-sent spirits
shine in the heaven
of eternal existence.
May all human souls
in the realm of earthly becoming
grow able to see
the light of their brilliance.

(Heidelberg, 21 January 1909[65])

For gradually developing esoteric sensitivity, especially, an effective meditation is to fill yourself before sleep with the feeling that you are now entering a world of spirit, a wonderful world of the gods where divine, spiritual beings of the higher hierarchies live and weave: they nurture and nourish you, sending their forces towards you and bearing you on their wings; and through them you are a power of the spiritual world, and they nurture you as a soul. E.D.N.
(Berlin, 25 April 1914[66])

In meditation, we should now consciously imitate the condition of sleep.
(Leipzig, 30 December 1913[67])

Waking life
In the universal spheres of spirit
stands the human being's spatial form.
In the universal realms of soul
weaves the human being's vital strength.

Sleeping life
In soul freedom's sphere
rests the human being's driving force.
In the realm of spirit sun,
the human power of thought creates.

(Notebook entry, end of December 1922[68])

In the evening reflect on this: during the night I will plunge into an invisible world, and will rest there. In this invisible world lies also the source of the highest virtues, especially the chief virtue—of love for all beings. I must continually draw anew from this source, for increasing perfection is only possible if the invisible is repeatedly led over into the visible. For this reason, the source of the visible can be found only in the invisible. All this must now be thought in images: I think of space filled with a light, the supersensible light of the divine, spiritual realm. I think of love as a warmth that streams through this supersensible world. And I think of myself resting at night in this supersensible world.

In the following seven lines, this is now pictured thus in the soul:

> In the godhead of the world
> I will find myself:
> I rest within it,
> the godliness of my soul shines out
> in pure love for every being;
> the godhead of the world gleams out
> in the pure rays of the light.

These seven lines, with their pictures should preoccupy your soul entirely for five minutes (measured intuitively, not by the clock). Then, for a further five minutes, erase all pictures from your mind and, maintaining complete inner tranquillity, give yourself up fully to the effect of these lines.

After this, do the review exercise, looking back on your day in reverse sequence.

In the morning, when you wake up, and before any other

impressions impinge on you, re-enliven the seven lines and their images, but now as follows:

> In the pure rays of the light
> gleams out the godhead of the world,
> in pure love for every being
> shines out the godliness of my soul;
> I rest in the godhead of the world,
> I will find myself
> in the godhead of the world.

Again, these seven lines must entirely preoccupy your awareness for five minutes, after which you should give yourself up entirely to their effect for a further five minutes, without any thought intruding.

After this, picture to yourself a growing plant, letting it develop very slowly in your thoughts leaf by leaf, then blossom, then fruit. Picture to yourself the force that propels this development. Then take this force into your own heart and concentrate on it there for two to three minutes.

(Handwritten note, undated[69])

Morning:
A white ray
of the bright sun
falls into my heart,
I grow strong
through the white ray:
thrice it strengthens
my I.

Evening:
Darkness,
spirit darkness
envelops me:
from the dark I will
receive the light,
the bright-dark light.

(For Hedwig Linnhoff, 1924[70])

Morning:
Radiant sun star,
luminous home
of world-shaping beings,
open up my heart
and sensing soul
so I may be vigorous
in time and eternity.

Evening:
To live in the spirit
and spiritually breathe
is the soul's impulse
and it will come to me when I
sleep, my eyes
closing protectively.

(For Mrs Roberts, November 1921[71])

Morning:
From the realm without feeling
I have entered the feeling realm.
I lived in the spirit
while I slept without feeling.
I live in sense
when I wake and feel.
I must call divine
both the realm without feeling
and the feeling one.
In God am I when awake,
and sleeping too I am
in God from whom I come
and to whom I return.

Evening:
To God from whom
I come, I return.
I am in him when asleep,
I am in him when awake.
Both the feeling realm
and the one without feeling
I must call divine.
I live in sense
when I wake and feel.
I live in spirit
when I sleep without feeling.
In sleep I enter
the realm without feeling:
the realm without feeling is
in the spirit.
Sleeping I will be
in the spirit.

(For a blind boy, undated[72])

In the breadths of the spatial world
brilliant light holds sway
so that things reveal themselves.
In the depths of the human heart
light becomes the power of thought
so that souls can live.

Light of the heart and light of the world:
God dwells in their finding
within offering human souls.
Thus lives the waking human being
in worlds of unfolding sense. - - -

In the breadths of the world of spirit
sense-extinguishing dark holds sway
so that the spirit can announce itself.
In the life of the human soul
darkness becomes God's brilliant light
so that human beings breathe the spirit.

Spirit of the soul and of the world divine:
in their finding the human being lives
within the grace and radiance of God.
Thus *sleeps* the soul
in worlds of unfolding spirit. - - -

When waking enters into slumber's twilight,
when *sleeping* enters into bright awakening,
then God's creation manifests
in cosmic-sensory revelation.

(For Father Giuseppe Trinchero, 9 September 1924[73])

Morning:
I see before me a white wall,
    upon which I write:
        I am.

I stand upon a blue surface—
    right foot: I press on the ground;
    left foot: the ground holds me up.

I am enclosed by a red-yellow firmament:
    the firmament encircles me and warms me
        I breathe in: ee
        I hold my breath within me: ah
        I breathe out: oh

Midday:
God's wisdom orders the world—
and also orders me;
I will live in it.
God's love warms the world—
and also warms my heart;
I will breathe in it.
God's strength carries the world—
and also carries my body;
I will think in it.

Evening:
It grows dark,
my soul goes into the dark
and will shine in the dark:
shine since wisdom, strength
and the goodness of God are within it;
wisdom, strength and goodness
grow in my soul in the dark—
through them my soul *wills*
to shine forth full of life again
through head and heart and limbs.

(For Maria Elsässer, summer 1921[74])

Morning and evening:
In the breadths of the world
soul strength works for every human being,
spirit power works for all souls.
    I will breathe soul strength,
    I will feel spirit power
    to be a human being filled with God.

(For Frau Renwald, July 1924[75])

Immediately after waking, before any sense impressions
impinge. Think nothing but this:

Self in the spirit.
you hold sway in the realm of the spheres,
you shine in the light,
you work in the fire,
you are wisdom, beauty, strength.
You are I.
I wish to be you.

(For Johanna Mücke, 1906[76]*)*

*The following thoughts should move very slowly through
the soul:*

Before me
in far distances
stands a star.
It comes ever closer toward me:
spirit beings
lovingly send me
the light of stars.
The star sinks down
into my own heart,
filling it with love:
the love in my heart
becomes in my soul
the strength to love.
I know that I
can also create in me
the strength to love.

(For Yvonne Gygax-Kraft, 1923[77])

Within me is an I that works from far breadths to near,
from near into far breadths.

Darkness: in the darkness, though, I find divine being.
Rose red: in the rose red I feel the source of all love.
Blue: in the blue of the ether the soul finds itself in
    devotion.
Green: in the green of life breathes the breath of all life.
Yellow: in the golden yellow shines thinking's clarity.
Red: in the red of fire will gathers its strength.
White: in sun-white the core of my being reveals itself.

(Handwritten note, 1908[78])

Night

	breathe in silently
I am in cosmic expanse—	breathe out
and expansive is my own being—	breathe in
my eye is the realm of heaven—	breathe out
and the ends of the life-threads	
(nerves)—	hold breath
are the stars—	breathe in slowly
the stars in my cosmic eye—	breathe out slowly
and my pupil is the moon—	hold breath
I see—	breathe out slowly
I see the firmament—	
and a point—	breathe out quickly
is the firmament—	breathe in quickly
The firmament is my soul—	hold breath
my I-bearing soul—	breathe out
	breathe in silently
	breathe out silently

(Notebook entry, 1923[79])

8. Verses and Prayers

Blue firmament,
deep blue,
star-strewn.

The moon moves across,
mild light shining from it:
mild light enters my forehead,
moonlight.

The sun sends it,
the moon makes it mild:
may it make me well.

(undated[80])

Like stars the god-sent spirits
shine in the heaven
of eternal existence.
May all human souls
in the realm of earthly becoming
grow able to see
the light of their brilliance.

(Heidelberg, 21 January 1909[81])

As from the blue ground of spirit
the gold-gleaming stars,
so from the depths of my soul
the strong powers that sustain me.

*(For Hermine Stein, on the death in battle of her son
Friedrich, on 22 March 1915[82])*

Christmas 1920

The soul of the earth is asleep
in summer's hot days:
the sun's bright mirror blazes
in outward space.

The soul of the earth awakens
in cold winter time:
and then the true sun shines
spiritually within.

In summer's joyful day,
earth sleeps deep;
in winter's holy night
earth rouses, wakes.

(For Helene Röchling, Christmas 1920[83])

See the universally active
eternal powers
of the stars in their stillness.

(Notebook entry, 1924[84])

Look into the realm of your soul,
and there you can feel
the powers of light of all the cosmic breadths
and the workings divine
of time's unfolding course.

Look into realms of sun and universe,
and there you can see
the spirit light of your own heart
and also the creative working
of your powers of soul.

Thus joyfully the human soul
can find in the depths of heart
cosmic, starry heights,
and the human eye
find in cosmic, starry heights
heart-deep spirit weaving.

(For Charlien Hupkes-Wegman, November 1924[85])

Into starry expanses,
toward the dwellings of the gods,
my soul turns
the gaze of spirit.

From starry expanses,
from dwellings of the gods,
streams the power of spirit
into my soul.

For starry expanses,
for dwellings of the gods,
lives *my* spirit's heart
through my soul.

(For Marie Steiner, Christmas 1924[86])

In tranquil quest
in light-aspiring
life of soul
my I bears me
toward the source
from which human beings
draw their true essence.

(Handwritten note, undated[87])

In the wide universe
weaves the true nature of the human being;
in the human core
is mirrored the image of the cosmos.
The I unites both, thus creating
the true meaning of existence.

(For Marie Hahn, autumn 1917[88])

In the far breadths you must learn
how only in the blue of ether distance
first vanishes cosmic existence,
before it finds itself in you again.

(Dornach, 8 December 1923[89])

Sun above me,
sun in the heavens' blue,
I on the star of earth:
green shines the earth
out into cosmic breadths.
The green of plants gives earth
one single green star colour.
Divine powers of metals
deep within gnome-homes, tinge
the starry blossoms red and blue and yellow
upon the green starflower ground.

(Handwritten note, undated[90])

The stars shine,
it is night:
stillness fills space,
all is quiet.
I feel the stillness,
I feel the silence.
In my heart,
in my head,
God speaks,
Christ speaks.

(For ten-year-old Nik Fiechter, June 1924[91])

From the stars I did come down.
To the stars will I raise myself aloft.
With Michael will I act.
For Christ will I live.

(For Alfred Meebold, undated[92])

Evening prayer

My heart gives thanks
that my eyes may see,
that my ears may hear,
that waking I may feel
in mother and father,
in all dear people,
in stars and clouds:
God's light,
God's love,
God's being;
that in sleep
these keep me safe
with their love, their light, their grace.

(For the children of the Heisler family, 2 June 1919[93])

Prayer at the ringing of evening bells

To wonder at beauty,
guard the truth,
honour what's noble,
resolve to do good:
this leads human beings
in life to their goal,
in deeds to what's right,
in feelings to peace,
in thinking to light;
and teaches them trust
in the workings of God,
in all that exists
in the universe,
in the innermost soul.

(For seven-year-old Pierre Grosheintz, 1913[94]*)*

Stars once spoke to us;
their silence now is world destiny:
awareness of the silence
can be suffering for our earthly being.

But in the silent stillness ripens
what we speak to the stars:
awareness of this speech
can strengthen our spirit being.

(For Marie Steiner, 25 December 1922[95])

Spiritual communion

In earth's workings, given in the reflection
of substances, the heavenly beings of stars
approach me:
I see them lovingly transform in will.
      I experience myself as soul.

In watery life, forming me through the forces
at work in substance, the heavenly deeds of stars
penetrate me.
I see them wisely transform in feeling.
      I experience myself as spirit.

(Dornach, 31 December 1922[96])

Christmas

At the crux of time
the spirit light of worlds entered
the stream of earthly being:
darkness of night
had held dominion,
bright light of day
shone into human souls—
light bringing warmth
to simple shepherd hearts;
light that illumines
kings' wise heads.
God-filled light,
Christ sun
O warm
our hearts,
illumine
our heads

so that good may be
all that we firmly
determine upon—
from the depths of our heart,
with the clarity of our heads.

(Dornach, 25 December 1923[97])

Notes

1. Lecture in Berlin, 20 February 1917, GA 175, p. 68.
2. Rudolf Steiner, *Knowledge of the Higher Worlds*, GA 10; and *Occult Science, An Outline*, GA 13.
3. Rudolf Steiner Press 2010.
4. GA 268, p. 171.
5. GA 233a, p. 162f.
6. GA 137, p. 136f.
7. GA 134, p. 11f.
8. GA 140, p. 145f.
9. GA 108, p. 116f.
10. GA 243, p. 44–6.
11. Ibid, p. 47.
12. GA 54, p. 26f.
13. GA 283, p. 40.
14. GA 121, p. 102f.
15. GA 268, p. 121.
16. GA 183, p. 87ff.
17. GA 103, p. 54.
18. GA 283, p. 22–4.
19. GA 218, p. 15f.
20. GA 175, p. 57f.
21. GA 193, p. 127.
22. GA 182, p. 143f.
23. GA 236, p. 276f.
24. Rudolf Steiner Archive, notebook page 5373, printed in GA 40, p. 331.
25. GA 105, p. 145f.

26. GA 95, p. 30.
27. GA 108, p. 51f.
28. GA 140, p. 80f.
29. GA 266c, p. 301.
30. GA 130, p. 87f.
31. GA 113, p. 30f.
32. GA 205, p. 203f.
33. GA 227, p. 171.
34. GA 102, p. 204
35. GA 266c, p. 299.
36. Whitsun verse, GA 40, p. 87.
37. GA 211, p. 17f.
38. GA 234, p. 56f.
39. GA 175, p. 68.
40. GA 240, p. 120.
41. Esoteric lesson, GA 266c, p. 300f. The asterisk marks what remains unspoken in esoteric meditation: Christ as the holiest, into whom we die.
42. GA 230, p. 132–4.
43. GA 182, p. 107f.
44. GA 268, p. 169.
45. GA 82, p. 85f.
46. GA 237, p. 46.
47. GA 140, p. 161.
48. GA 276, p. 76–9.
49. Ibid, p. 79–81.
50. GA 176, p. 48.
51. GA 218, p. 22.
52. Translator's note: The German text says 'twelve fixed stars'.
53. GA 214, p. 179–81.
54. GA 226, p. 47f.

55. GA 40, p. 41.
56. GA 236, p. 245–7.
57. GA 125, p. 247f.
58. GA 125, p. 257f.
59. GA 127, p. 223f.
60. GA 223, p. 28f.
61. GA 96, p. 189–92.
62. GA 158, p. 170.
63. GA 219, p. 36f.
64. GA 40, p. 97.
65. GA 40, p. 113.
66. GA 266c, p. 304. The abbreviation at the end stands for Ex Deo Nascimur.
67. GA 266c, p. 239.
68. GA 40, p. 148.
69. Rudolf Steiner Archive, notebook page 4462–4, printed in GA 267, p. 184f.
70. GA 268, p. 176.
71. GA 268, p. 158.
72. GA 268, p. 189.
73. GA 268, p. 104f.
74. GA 268, p. 156f.
75. GA 268, p. 102.
76. GA 268, p. 25.
77. GA 268, p. 91.
78. Rudolf Steiner Archive, notebook page 7169, printed in GA 268, p. 35.
79. GA 267, p. 454.
80. Transcribed by Elisabeth Steffen, GA 268, p. 177.
81. GA 40, p. 113.
82. GA 268, p. 211.

83. GA 40, p. 105.
84. GA 40, p. 170.
85. GA 268, p. 110.
86. GA 268, p. 111.
87. Rudolf Steiner Archive, notebook page 3920, printed in GA 268, p. 121.
88. GA 40, p. 278.
89. GA 40, p. 179.
90. Rudolf Steiner Archive, notebook page 4449, printed in GA 268, p. 120.
91. GA 268, p. 171.
92. GA 268, p. 120.
93. GA 40, p. 239.
94. GA 40, p. 234.
95. GA 40, p. 107.
96. GA 268, p. 259.
97. GA 40, p. 108f.

Sources

The following volumes are cited in this book. Where relevant, published editions of equivalent English translations are provided.

The works of Rudolf Steiner are listed with the volume numbers of the complete works in German, the *Gesamtausgabe* (GA), as published by Rudolf Steiner Verlag, Dornach, Switzerland.

RSP = Rudolf Steiner Press, UK
AP / SB = Anthroposophic Press / SteinerBooks, USA

GA

10   *Knowledge of the Higher Worlds* (RSP) / *How to Know Higher Worlds* (SB)

13   *Occult Science* (RSP) / *An Outline of Esoteric Science* (SB)

40   *Wahrspruchworte*

54   *Die Welträtsel und die Anthroposophie*

82   *Damit der Mensch ganz Mensch werde*

95   *Founding a Science of the Spirit* (RSP)

96   *Original Impulses for the Science of the Spirit* (Completion Press)

102   *Good and Evil Spirits* (RSP)

103   *The Gospel of St John* (AP)

105   *Universe, Earth and Man* (RSP)

108   *Die Beantwortung von Welt- und Lebensfragen durch Anthroposophie*

113   *The East in the Light of the West* (RSP)

121   *The Mission of the Individual Folk Souls* (RSP)

125   *Paths and Goals of the Spiritual Human Being* (RSP)

All English-language titles are available via Rudolf Steiner Press, UK (www.rudolfsteinerpress.com) or SteinerBooks, USA (www.steinerbooks.org)

A NOTE FROM RUDOLF STEINER PRESS

We are an independent publisher and registered charity (non-profit organisation) dedicated to making available the work of Rudolf Steiner in English translation. We care a great deal about the content of our books and have hundreds of titles available – as printed books, ebooks and in audio formats.

As a publisher devoted to anthroposophy...

- We continually commission translations of previously unpublished works by Rudolf Steiner and invest in re-translating, editing and improving our editions.

- We are committed to making anthroposophy available to all by publishing introductory books as well as contemporary research.

- Our new print editions and ebooks are carefully checked and proofread for accuracy, and converted into all formats for all platforms.

- Our translations are officially authorised by Rudolf Steiner's estate in Dornach, Switzerland, to whom we pay royalties on sales, thus assisting their critical work.

So, look out for Rudolf Steiner Press as a mark of quality and support us today by buying our books, or contact us should you wish to sponsor specific titles or to support the charity with a gift or legacy.

office@rudolfsteinerpress.com
Join our e-mailing list at www.rudolfsteinerpress.com

RUDOLF STEINER PRESS